Title:

secret ways to overcoming procrastination for teens:

Copyright

All rights reserved. No part of this publication may be reproduced, distributed, or transmitted in any form or by any means, including photocopying, recording, or other electronic or mechanical methods, without the prior written permission of the publisher, except in the case of brief quotations embodied in critical reviews and certain other noncommercial uses permitted by copyright law.

Copyright © (Peterson Caleb), (2024).

Introduction

Overcome Smash Hour: Opening the Distinct advantages Against Lingering for Adolescents

Is your plan for the day a beast under your bed, becoming greater as time passes? Do cutoff times loom like shadows, creeping you out? Dread not, individual youngster hero! This book is your unmistakable advantage against the feared monster of hesitation.

Disregard exhausting talks and reused guidance. Plunge into a **battle plan made explicitly for YOU**, loaded with **insider tips, ninja moves, and stowed away knowledge** to crush your stalling evil spirits. Find:

The foundation of your procrastination: Expose the subtle lowlifes attacking your concentration and efficiency.
Cerebrum hacks for extreme control: Figure out how to outfox your own psyche and release your internal efficiency monster.
Using time effectively mastery: Specialty schedules that work for YOU, not against you. Express farewell to dusk 'til dawn affairs and hi to calm achievement.
The force of "simply doing it": Find the enchantment of beginning little and gathering speed to overcome even the most overwhelming errands.
Stalling prevention: Construct mental strongholds to oppose interruptions and remain on track like a laser.
Extra journeys and challenges: Put your newly discovered abilities under serious scrutiny with intuitive activities and certifiable difficulties.

This book is something other than an aide; it's your **personal delaying busting companion**. Loaded up with engaging stories, humor, and significant guidance, it will be your team promoter, mentor, and clear-cut advantage in the battle against time-squandering mythical serpents.

Quit feeling overpowered and begin accomplishing your goals! Look up, click "Purchase Now," and join the positions of relentless adolescents who vanquish their days and crush their objectives. Keep in mind, stalling doesn't have an opportunity against a high schooler furnished with the right information and the will to win!

** Don't pause! Hesitating on purchasing this book is simply giving tarrying more power.

Table of contents

Understanding procrastination
Time management techniques
Setting realistic goals
Building proactive mindset
Dealing with distractions
Developing a consistent routine
Overcoming perfectionism
Mindfulness and focus
Utilizing technology wisely
Balance work and play

Understanding procrastination

Delaying, a widespread test, rises above age, occupation, and social limits. At its center, dawdling includes the postponement or aversion of errands notwithstanding monitoring their significance or likely outcomes. This apparently nonsensical way of behaving is well established in human brain science and is a mind boggling transaction of different variables.

One vital component in understanding hesitation is perceiving the perplexing equilibrium inside the human mind. The cerebrum frequently wrestles with the pressure between the quick delight of staying away from an undertaking and the drawn out advantages of finishing it. This battle is a consequence of the cerebrum's inclination for moment delight, looking for guaranteed compensations over deferred, however frequently more huge, gains.

Anxiety toward disappointment is another strong power driving hesitation. The fear of not living up to assumptions or delivering inferior outcomes can deaden. This dread turns into an impressive obstruction, driving people to put off errands as a method for protecting themselves from expected dissatisfaction or analysis.

Inspiration, or the deficiency in that department, assumes a significant part in tarrying. At the point when assignments appear to be overpowering or need inherent allure, people might battle to call the drive expected to start and finish them. The shortfall of an unmistakable feeling of direction or excitement for an errand can add to the delaying peculiarity.

Unfortunate using time effectively fuels lingering, as people might wind up wrecked by the sheer volume of errands or incapable to really focus on. The absence of an organized arrangement frequently brings about a pattern of stalling, making a self-building up design that can be trying to break.

Figuring out delaying, in this manner, includes recognizing these mental and social subtleties. By disentangling the complexities of the hesitation puzzle, people gain mindfulness, preparing for designated intercessions and the execution of systems to defeat this unavoidable test. Eventually, understanding hesitation is a vital stage towards developing a proactive mentality and cultivating propensities that lead to further developed efficiency and prosperity.

Time management techniques

Viable using time effectively is essential for accomplishing objectives, diminishing pressure, and upgrading by and large efficiency. Different strategies can help people in dominating this ability:

Prioritization: Recognize errands in view of desperation and significance utilizing strategies like the Eisenhower Lattice. Focus on high-influence assignments for better time usage.

To-Do Lists: Make records to sort out errands and give a visual guide. Tick off finished things for a feeling of achievement.

Time Blocking: Allot explicit time blocks to various exercises. This cutoff points performing different errands and updates base on every single endeavor.

Pomodoro Technique: Work in centered stretches, commonly 25 minutes, trailed by a brief break. Rehash the cycle to keep up with focus and forestall burnout.

Set Savvy Goals: Characterize Explicit, Quantifiable, Feasible, Pertinent, and Time-bound objectives. This clearness helps in successful preparation and execution.

Batching: Gather comparative assignments and tackle them during committed schedule openings. This limits setting exchanging and further develops effectiveness.

Utilize a Calendar: Use schedules to plan errands, arrangements, and cutoff times. This gives a visual outline of responsibilities.

Kill Distractions: Recognize and diminish interruptions like warnings, pointless gatherings, or useless conditions.

Time Auditing: Track how time is gone through over the course of the day. This assists in relating to timing squandering exercises and regions for development.

Lay out Routines: Foster reliable everyday schedules. Unsurprising examples make structure and further develop using time effectively.

Figure out how to Say No: Be specific about responsibilities. Expressing no to extra undertakings that don't line up with needs forestalls overcommitment.

Cutoff time Awareness: Set sensible cutoff times and remain mindful of looming dates. This forestalls last-minute surges and improves arranging.

Use Innovation Wisely: Influence efficiency applications and apparatuses for task the board, updates, and time following.

Normal Breaks: Consolidate brief breaks during work to invigorate and re-energize. This forestalls burnout and keeps up with center.

Delegate Tasks: Whenever the situation allows, delegate errands to other people. Appointing can ease up the responsibility and take into consideration more productive time use.

By embracing a mix of these time usage methods, people can make an organized and viable way to deal with their day to day undertakings, at last prompting expanded efficiency and a superior balance between serious and fun activities.

Setting realistic goals

Defining sensible objectives is a principal part of powerful using time effectively and individual accomplishment. Sensible objectives are those that are both testing and feasible inside a given time period. Here are key standards and procedures for laying out practical objectives:

Specificity: Obviously characterize your objective. Unclear goals make it challenging to make an engaged arrangement and measure progress. Be exact about what you need to accomplish.

Measurability: Lay out rules for estimating progress. Quantifiable measurements give lucidity and assist with following your progression toward the objective.

Achievability: Survey whether the objective is sensibly feasible. Think about your assets, abilities, and time imperatives. A difficult objective is rousing, yet it ought to stay reachable.

Relevance: Guarantee that the objective lines up with your more extensive goals and values. An objective ought to add to your general vision and be significant with regards to your life.

Time-bound: Set a cutoff time for accomplishing the objective. This adds a need to get going and helps in arranging and focusing on errands really.

Break it Down: Separation bigger objectives into more modest, sensible errands. This makes the objective more reachable as well as gives an unmistakable guide to advance.

Think about Constraints: Perceive any possible deterrents or imperatives that could obstruct your advancement. Understanding difficulties ahead of time takes into consideration better readiness and critical thinking.

Consider Resources: Survey the assets expected to achieve the objective. Whether now is the ideal time, abilities, or outside help, understanding your necessities works with powerful preparation.

Flexibility: While setting explicit cutoff times is essential, take into account some adaptability. Life is dynamic, and unforeseen occasions might influence your timetable. Versatility is critical to exploring changes.

Observe Milestones: Recognize and celebrate more modest accomplishments en route. Perceiving progress helps inspiration and supports your obligation to the bigger objective.

Input Loop: Consistently survey and rethink your objectives. Request input from yourself or others to measure headway and make changes if necessary.

Gain from Setbacks: Comprehend that mishaps are a characteristic piece of the objective setting process. Rather than review them as disappointments, consider them to be chances to learn and straighten out your system.

By integrating these standards into objective setting, people can develop a sensible and compelling way to deal with accomplishing their desires. This technique advances accomplishment as well as improves inspiration and self-assurance chasing after private and expert targets.

Building proactive mindset

Building a proactive outlook includes developing a proactive way to deal with life, where people step up, expect difficulties, and effectively look for arrangements. Here are systems to encourage a proactive mentality:

Self-Awareness: Grasp your assets, shortcomings, values, and objectives. Mindfulness frames the establishment for going with deliberate choices and making intentional moves.

Positive Attitude: Embrace an inspirational perspective, seeing difficulties as any open doors for development as opposed to obstructions. A positive mentality fills proactive way of behaving.

Drive Taking: Effectively look for amazing chances to step up to the plate. Trusting that things will happen can prompt a responsive mentality, while proactivity includes getting things going.

Objective Setting: Characterize clear and reachable objectives. Proactively setting targets gives an internal compass and inspiration, propelling you to make reliable moves.

Adaptability: Embrace change and view it as a steady throughout everyday life. Being versatile empowers you to explore unforeseen circumstances with flexibility and inventiveness.

Critical thinking Skills: Foster compelling critical thinking abilities. Rather than harping on issues, center around tracking down arrangements and doing whatever it may take to address difficulties.

Time Management: Proactively deal with your time by focusing on errands, defining objectives, and making plans. This forestalls tarrying and guarantees an emphasis on what makes the biggest difference.

Nonstop Learning: Develop a mentality of constant learning and improvement. Remain inquisitive, look for new information, and effectively seek after potential open doors for individual and expert turn of events.

Resilience: Construct versatility to return quickly from misfortunes. Proactive people view disappointments as brief misfortunes, gaining from them and utilizing the experience to fuel future achievement.

Organizing and Collaboration: Proactively interface with others, share thoughts, and team up. Building serious areas of strength for a cultivates a steady climate that energizes proactive undertakings.

Dynamic Confidence: Trust your capacity to decide. A proactive outlook includes conclusiveness and trust in picking a game-plan.

**Responsibility for: Assume a sense of ownership with your activities and results. Proactively possessing your choices engages you to gain from encounters and develop.

Visualization: Envision achievement and the means expected to accomplish your objectives. This psychological practice supports a proactive outlook by making a reasonable image of your ideal results.

Appreciation Practice: Develop appreciation to see the value in the positive parts of your life. A thankful outlook can upgrade by and large prosperity and inspiration.

Building a proactive mentality is a continuous interaction that includes purposeful decisions and steady activities. By integrating these methodologies into day to day existence, people can foster a proactive methodology, prompting better progress, satisfaction, and strength despite challenges.

Dealing with distractions

Really managing interruptions is vital for keeping up with concentration and efficiency. Here are procedures to limit interruptions:

Make a Devoted Workspace: Lay out an assigned region for work or study to flag the beginning of centered exercises and limit outside unsettling influences.

Switch Off Notifications: Quietness or mood killer pointless warnings on your gadgets to keep away from steady interferences.

Set Clear Boundaries: Convey your requirement for continuous chance to everyone around you, laying out limits during explicit work periods.

Focus on Tasks: Recognize and focus on assignments to guarantee you focus on the main exercises, decreasing the effect of interruptions.

Time Blocking: Apportion explicit time blocks for various errands. During these blocks, center exclusively around the alloted action, limiting the impulse to perform multiple tasks or get occupied.

Use Efficiency Tools: Use applications or devices intended to support efficiency by impeding diverting sites or assisting you with keeping focused with your undertakings.

Separate Tasks: Gap bigger undertakings into more modest, more sensible advances. This can cause the work to appear to be less overpowering and assist with keeping up with center.

Carry out the Pomodoro Technique: Work to put it plainly, engaged stretches (e.g., 25 minutes) trailed by a concise break. This strategy oversees interruptions and keep up with focus.

Wear Headphones: Use earphones to indicate to others that you're in an engaged state. They can likewise assist with limiting surrounding commotion and establish a more focused climate.

Set Explicit Work Hours: Lay out unambiguous work hours and impart them to associates, companions, or family to limit surprising interferences.

Practice Mindfulness: Consolidate care procedures to prepare your psyche to remain present and zeroed in on the main job, decreasing powerlessness to interruptions.

Arrange Your Space: Keep your actual work area clean and coordinated. A messiness free climate can decrease visual interruptions and make a more favorable environment for focus.

Plan Breaks: Plan brief breaks during your work meetings to revive your psyche. This can help forestall burnout and keep up with supported center when you return to your errands.

Lay out Rituals: Create pre-work or pre-concentrate on ceremonies to flag the beginning of centered exercises, making a psychological progress away from possible interruptions.

Use Don't Upset Mode: Initiate the Don't Upset mode on your gadgets during basic work periods to limit approaching calls or messages.

Steady execution of these systems can essentially upgrade your capacity to oversee interruptions, encouraging a more engaged and useful work or review climate.

Developing a consistent routine

Fostering a reliable routine is a strong procedure for improving efficiency and generally prosperity. This is an aide while heading to lay out and keep a predictable daily schedule:

 Set Clear Goals: Characterize your present moment and long haul objectives. Your routine ought to line up with these targets to guarantee engaged and intentional day to day exercises.

Distinguish Priorities: Decide the main assignments and obligations in your day to day existence. Center around these needs while organizing your daily schedule.

Lay out a Morning Routine: Begin your day with a steady morning schedule. This could incorporate exercises like awakening simultaneously, exercise, reflection, or a nutritious breakfast.

Make a Schedule: Foster an everyday timetable that frames explicit time allotments for work, study, dinners, exercise, and unwinding. Adhere to this timetable as intently as could really be expected.

Focus on Self-Care: Remember taking care of oneself exercises for your daily schedule, like adequate rest, quality dinners, and breaks. Dealing with your physical and mental prosperity is essential for keeping up with consistency.

Limit Choice Fatigue: Limit direction by arranging your daily practice ahead of time. This lessens pressure and assists you with adhering to your timetable all the more easily.

Incorporate Support Time: Consider cushion time between exercises to represent unforeseen deferrals or changes. This forestalls feeling hurried and overpowered.

Be Realistic: Guarantee your routine is sensible and manageable. Defining excessively aggressive objectives might prompt burnout, so figure out some kind of harmony that suits your way of life.

Predictable Rest Patterns: Keep up with reliable rest and wake times, as a very much managed rest design decidedly influences your energy levels and by and large wellbeing.

Survey and Adjust: Consistently audit your everyday practice to evaluate its adequacy. Be available to changes in light of changing conditions or objectives.

Consolidate Breaks: Incorporate brief breaks into your everyday practice to re-energize your brain. Short delays can upgrade center and forestall burnout.

End of the week Planning: Plan your ends of the week somewhat, keeping a harmony among unwinding and efficiency. This keeps up with consistency in any event, during less organized days.

Use Technology: Influence innovation, like alerts or updates, to provoke advances among exercises and keep you on target.

Remain Flexible: While consistency is vital, be versatile to unforeseen changes. Life is dynamic, and being too unbending may prompt dissatisfaction. Adaptability is a fundamental part of a manageable daily practice.

Observe Achievements: Recognize and commend your accomplishments, regardless of how little. Encouraging feedback can propel you to adhere to your daily schedule.

Overcoming perfectionism

Beating compulsiveness is an excursion towards embracing defect, overseeing assumptions, and encouraging a better outlook. Here are systems to assist with conquering compulsiveness:

Set Sensible Standards: Lay out feasible and reasonable norms for yourself. Comprehend that flawlessness is impossible, and setting unreasonably exclusive requirements can be counterproductive.

Perceive Negative Thoughts: Recognize and challenge negative contemplations related with hairsplitting. Supplant self-basic proclamations with additional practical and merciful ones.

Observe Progress, Not Simply Results: Recognize and commend the headway you make, regardless of whether you accomplish flawlessness. Stress the work and development engaged with the interaction.

Acknowledge Imperfections: Embrace the possibility that no one's perfect and has defects. Tolerating your defects is a urgent move toward beating hairsplitting.

Break Undertakings into More modest Steps: Separation bigger assignments into more modest, more reasonable advances. This approach gains it simpler to zero in on headway as opposed flawlessly.

Gain from Mistakes: View botches as any open doors for learning and development instead of as disappointments. Break down what turned out badly, separate examples, and apply them in later undertakings.

Set Time Limits: Assign explicit measures of time for errands to forestall overthinking and extreme refinement. Setting practical time limits energizes productivity.

Challenge the Requirement for Approval: Look at whether your compulsiveness is driven by a longing for outside approval. Center around inner fulfillment and self-endorsement all things considered.

Focus on Self-Care: Practice self-sympathy and focus on taking care of oneself. Dealing with your physical and mental prosperity adds to a more adjusted point of view.

Change Your Language: Supplant outright terms like "consistently" or "never" with more moderate language. This makes a more practical and adaptable mentality.

Look for Input and Support: Offer your objectives and progress with others. Looking for input and support can give important viewpoints and reduce the strain of flawlessness.

Care and Unwinding Techniques: Integrate care or unwinding methods into your everyday practice. These practices can assist with overseeing nervousness and fussbudget propensities.

Rethink Success: Shift your meaning of achievement from flawlessness to ceaseless improvement. Embrace the possibility that advancement and development are marks of achievement.

Lay out Boundaries: Put down stopping points to forestall overcommitting yourself. Comprehend that it's alright to say no and focus on errands in view of their significance.

Appreciation Practice: Develop appreciation for what you have achieved. An appreciation practice assists shift with centering away based on what's missing and encourages a positive mentality.

Beating compulsiveness is a continuous cycle that includes self-reflection, self-empathy, and the steady reception of better viewpoints. By executing these systems, people can foster a more adjusted and reasonable way to deal with their objectives and tries.

Mindfulness and focus

Care is a strong practice that can fundamentally improve concentration and generally speaking prosperity. This is the way care adds to further developed center:

Present Second Awareness: Care includes focusing on the current second without judgment. By zeroing in on the now, people can keep their psyches from meandering into interruptions or worries about the past or future.

Decreasing Mental Clutter: Care helps clear mental mess by advancing a non-critical consciousness of considerations and sentiments. This psychological lucidity takes into consideration further developed fixation on the main job.

Developing Concentration: Care reflection frequently includes focusing on a particular point of convergence, like the breath. This training fortifies the capacity to think and supports center after some time.

Stress Reduction: Care is related with pressure decrease, which can be a huge consider further developing concentration. By overseeing pressure, people are better ready to guide their focus toward the current second.

Improved Self-Regulation: Care supports self-guideline by elevating a cognizant reaction to boosts instead of imprudent responses. This mindfulness adds to all the more likely command over consideration and concentration.

Careful Breathing: Zeroing in on the breath is a typical care strategy. This straightforward practice helps anchor thoughtfulness regarding the current second, encouraging a quiet and focused state helpful for centered exercises.

Body Sweep Meditation: Care based body examine contemplations include focusing on various pieces of the body. This training upgrades mindfulness and can work on the capacity to focus on unambiguous assignments.

Careful Walking: Taking part in careful strolling includes focusing on each step and the sensations related with strolling. This training advances establishing and can be a reviving break during work or study meetings.

Acknowledgment of Distractions: As opposed to opposing interruptions, care empowers recognizing them without judgment and tenderly directing consideration back to the planned concentration. This acknowledgment oversees interferences all the more really.

Worked on Profound Regulation: Care cultivates close to home guideline, keeping close to home interruptions from wrecking center. By noticing feelings non-critically, people can keep a more clear mental space for undertakings.

Careful Listening: Rehearsing careful listening includes completely captivating in the demonstration of tuning in without permitting the brain to meander. This expertise can upgrade center during discussions or while handling data.

By integrating care rehearses into day to day schedules, people can develop an uplifted feeling of mindfulness, lessen the effect of interruptions, and foster a more engaged and purposeful way to deal with their exercises. Normal care practice can prompt long haul enhancements in consideration and focus.

Utilizing technology wisely

Using innovation shrewdly is significant for boosting its advantages while limiting possible downsides. Here are procedures to guarantee shrewd and careful utilization of innovation:

Set Innovation Boundaries: Lay out unambiguous time limits for innovation use to forestall over the top screen time. Characterize periods for work, recreation, and unwinding to keep up with balance.

Use Efficiency Apps: Influence efficiency applications and devices to sort out assignments, set updates, and oversee time really. Applications like schedules, plans for the day, and undertaking the board apparatuses can upgrade proficiency.

Cluster Notifications: Timetable explicit times to browse and answer messages,

messages, and warnings. Grouping these exercises diminishes interferences and further develops center during devoted work or study meetings.

Advanced Detox Periods: Assign ordinary computerized detox periods, during which you detach from electronic gadgets. This break takes into consideration mental revival and diminishes reliance on innovation.

Focus on Significant Tasks: Use innovation to focus on and tackle significant assignments first. This guarantees that innovation fills in as a device for efficiency as opposed to a wellspring of interruption.

Set Gadget Free Zones: Assign specific regions, like the room or feasting region, as gadget free zones. This advances better relational associations and keeps innovation from infringing on private spaces.

Careful Online Entertainment Use: Be aware of virtual entertainment utilization. Set time limits for web-based entertainment commitment, unfollow accounts that add to pessimism, and curate a positive web-based climate.

Mechanize Tedious Tasks: Investigate mechanization apparatuses to smooth out dull assignments. This can save time and permit you to zero in on additional significant and complex exercises.

Routinely Update Apps: Keep your product and applications cutting-edge to guarantee ideal usefulness and security. Standard updates frequently incorporate enhancements that add to a smoother client experience.

Learn Console Shortcuts: Find out more about console alternate routes for programming and applications. This can fundamentally increment effectiveness and lessen dependence on the mouse, saving time.

Assess Application Usage: Intermittently audit the applications on your gadgets. Eliminate superfluous or seldom utilized applications to clean up and smooth out your computerized space.

Use Don't Upset Mode: Enact the Don't Upset mode during centered work or study meetings. This quiets notices, limiting interruptions and advancing concentrated exertion.

Secure Your Advanced Space: Carry areas of strength for out and utilize security highlights like two-factor validation to safeguard your computerized protection. Consistently update passwords for added security.

Careful Substance Consumption: Consume online substance carefully. Be specific about the data you draw in with and guarantee it lines up with your objectives and values.

Instruct Yourself: Remain informed about the most recent advanced patterns, protection settings, and safety efforts. Being educated permits you to successfully explore the advanced scene more.

By taking on these procedures, people can bridle the force of innovation for efficiency, remain aware of its effect on prosperity, and develop a fair and purposeful way to deal with computerized use.

Balance work and play

Adjusting work and play is fundamental for generally speaking prosperity and supported efficiency. Here are systems to accomplish a solid harmony between proficient obligations and recreation exercises:

Lay out Priorities: Obviously characterize your work and individual needs. Understanding what makes the biggest difference assists in assigning with timing really.

Set Boundaries: Make clear limits among work and individual time. Try not to allow work to infringe into your relaxation hours as well as the other way around.

Make a Schedule: Foster an efficient timetable that incorporates assigned time for work errands, breaks, and relaxation exercises.

Adhere to your timetable to keep up with balance.

Focus on Self-Care: Focus on taking care of oneself. Guarantee you get adequate rest, exercise, and unwinding to re-energize your energy for both work and play.

Use Innovation Mindfully: Influence innovation to improve efficiency during work hours, however be aware of its effect on private time. Put down certain boundaries on business related warnings during recreation hours.

Take Standard Breaks: Integrate brief breaks into your work routine to forestall burnout. Utilize these breaks to take part in exercises you appreciate, advancing a reasonable way of life.

Plan Relaxation Activities: Timetable pleasant recreation exercises as you would work gatherings. This guarantees that individual time is given similar degree of significance as expert responsibilities.

Learn to Say No: Be specific about taking on extra work responsibilities. Figuring out how to say no when essential keeps a good arrangement among work and play.

Weekend Planning: Plan your ends of the week to incorporate a blend of unwinding, social exercises, and individual interests. This approach adds to a balanced and fulfilling break.

Time Blocking: Use time impeding to assign explicit blocks for work, play, and different responsibilities. This technique helps in picturing and keeping an equilibrium in your day to day plan.

Delegate When Possible: If plausible, delegate errands at work and offer liabilities in your own life. Appointing disseminates the responsibility and makes additional opportunity for recreation.

Keep away from Perfectionism: Acknowledge that flawlessness isn't attainable all the time. Taking a stab at flawlessness in both work and individual life can prompt pressure and unevenness.

Participate in Hobbies: Commit time to leisure activities and exercises you appreciate. Taking part in imaginative or sporting pursuits adds to a feeling of satisfaction beyond work.

Quality Over Quantity: Spotlight on the nature of your work and relaxation time instead of the amount. Significant and centered commitment is more important than sheer volume.

Customary Reflection: Consistently consider your balance between serious and fun activities. Change your methodology depending on the situation, taking into account changes in needs or obligations.

Adjusting work and play is a continuous cycle that requires mindfulness and purposeful navigation. By consolidating these methodologies, people can lead a really satisfying life that blends proficient accomplishments with individual prosperity.

Printed in Great Britain
by Amazon